King Arthur's Tale

Anita Ganeri

Published 2011 by
A&C Black Publishers Ltd.
36 Soho Square, London, W1D 3QY

www.acblack.com

ISBN HB 978-1-4081-3382-8
      PB 978-1-4081-3377-4

Text copyright © 2010 Anita Ganeri

This book is produced using paper that is made from wood grown in managed, sustainable forests. It is natural, renewable and recyclable. The logging and manufacturing processes conform to the environmental regulations of the country of origin.

Produced for A&C Black by Calcium. www.calciumcreative.co.uk

Printed and bound in China by C&C Offset Printing Co.

All the internet addresses given in this book were correct at the time of going to press. The author and publishers regret any inconvenience caused if addresses have changed or sites have ceased to exist, but can accept no responsibility for any such changes.

Acknowledgements

The publishers would like to thank the following for their kind permission to reproduce their photographs:

Cover: Shutterstock.
Pages: Corbis: Jonathan Hession/Touchstone/Bureau L.A. Collection 4, Lebrecht Music & Arts 12, Fred de Noyelle/Godong 15; Dreamstime: Matthew Collingwood 21, Philcold 20, Lynn Woodward 17; Getty: Fine Art Photographic 19; Shutterstock: Linda Bucklin 3, 16, Graham De'ath 1, 13, Diligent 8, Michael Hansen 10, André Klaassen 6, Papa 14, Raulin 18, Sergood 11, Ljupco Smokovski 9, Serghei Starus 7, Yuri Tuchkov 5.

Contents

King Arthur

Long ago, there lived a man called Arthur who was a great king of Britain. He was also a brave and brilliant **knight**.

A knight's tale

I, Lancelot, was Arthur's friend and one of his knights. I am going to tell you the story of Arthur's life – it is a story filled with adventure.

 Arthur had a group of **loyal** knights.

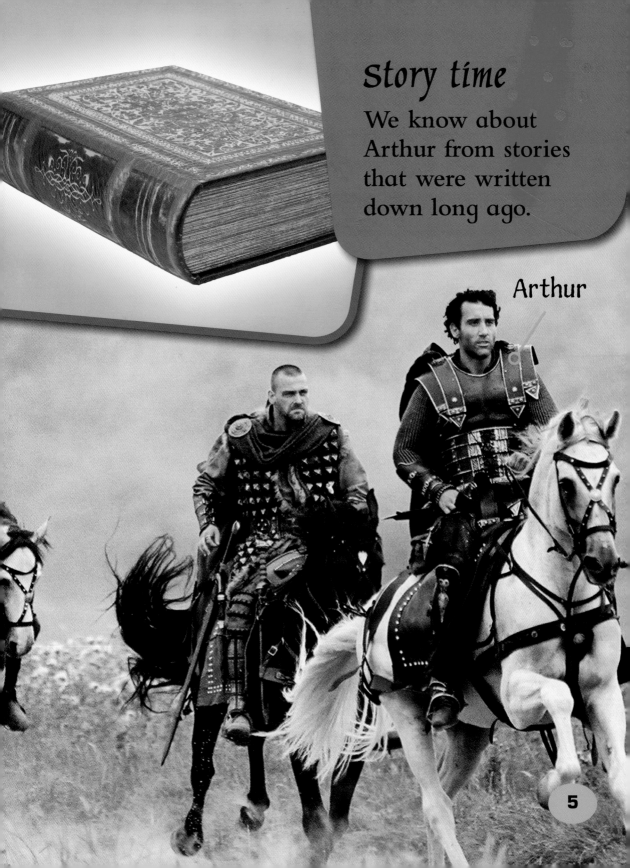

Story time

We know about Arthur from stories that were written down long ago.

Arthur

Arthur is Born

Arthur was born in a great castle called Tintagel Castle, in **Cornwall**. His father was a powerful king and fighter called Uther Pendragon.

Sent away

When Arthur was born, Uther told a **wizard** called Merlin to look after him. Arthur was then sent to live with a knight called Sir Ector and grew up with his family.

Merlin

Merlin was a wizard who could do **magic**. He was Arthur's teacher and friend.

Arthur was born in a great castle, like this one.

The Sword in the Stone

Then King Uther died, but no one knew he had a son because Uther had sent Arthur away when he was born. People began to **argue** about who should be king.

Who is strong enough?

One day, Arthur saw a sword stuck into a large stone. It was said that anyone who could pull out the sword would be king. Arthur pulled it out easily!

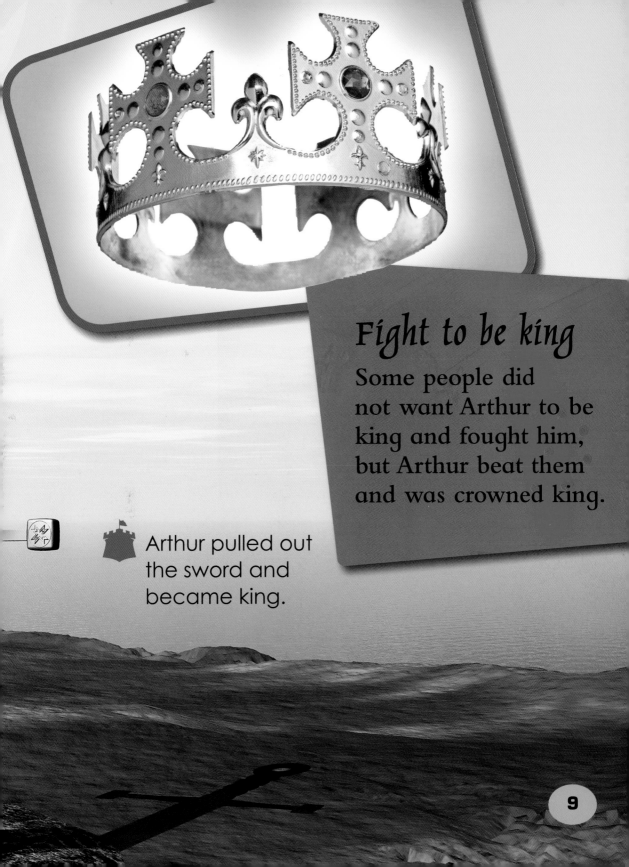

Fight to be king

Some people did not want Arthur to be king and fought him, but Arthur beat them and was crowned king.

Arthur pulled out the sword and became king.

Excalibur!

One day Merlin took Arthur to a magical lake where the Lady of the Lake lived. She gave Arthur a wonderful sword.

Keep Arthur safe

The sword was called Excalibur. When Arthur wore the sword's **scabbard**, it was impossible for him to be hurt in a fight.

 When Arthur fought with the sword, he always won.

Excalibur

Silver sword

Excalibur was made of silver and was covered with beautiful jewels. The sword's blade was very sharp.

Marry Me!

When he became king, Arthur lived in a castle at a place called Camelot. It stood by a river and was surrounded by lots of green forests.

Arthur's wedding

Soon after he had become king, Arthur met and fell in love with a princess, called Guinevere. She was the daughter of King Leodegrance. Arthur and Guinevere got married.

Round table

Round table

Guinevere's father gave her and Arthur a huge round table as a wedding present.

 Guinevere was beautiful and kind.

Arthur's Knights

Arthur's most trusted knights were allowed to sit at the round table. They were called the Knights of the Round Table.

Brave knights

Some of the bravest knights were Galahad, Percival, and Bors. I, Lancelot, was one of Arthur's Knights of the Round Table.

The knights were brave and daring fighters.

Round about

There was no top seat at the round table, so everyone had an **equal** place.

Adventures

Arthur fought the Saxons, who were attacking Britain. This made the people safe again and Arthur was seen as a great king.

Dragons and princesses

Arthur and his knights fought dragons and **evil** knights. They **rescued** beautiful princesses and some knights searched for a special cup called the '**Holy Grail**'.

 Dragons could breathe fire!

We will rule

The Saxons were fighters from Germany and Denmark who wanted to **rule** all of Britain.

Saxon

Last Fight

Mordred was Arthur's evil **nephew**. He wanted to be king, and was determined to fight and kill Arthur so that he could take his crown.

Arthur was hurt

Arthur fought Mordred at the Battle of Camlan. He killed Mordred, but he was badly hurt because he was not wearing Excalibur's scabbard.

 Arthur and his knights fought a brave battle.

Wicked sister

Excalibur's scabbard had been stolen by Mordred's mother, and Arthur's sister, Morgan Le Fay.

Morgan Le Fay

Arthur Dies

After the battle, Arthur was ill. He knew he was dying, so he told a knight called Bedivere to throw Excalibur back into the magical lake.

Magical island

Then a boat took King Arthur to the magical island of **Avalon**. Soon afterwards, Arthur died there, but no one knows where he was buried.

Avalon

This is a place called Glastonbury. Some people think that it was once Avalon.

Excalibur

The Lady of the Lake took back Excalibur, to keep the sword safe in the lake forever.

Glossary

argue fight about something

Avalon magical island surrounded by mist

Cornwall the south-western tip of Britain

equal the same amount of importance

evil very bad or wicked

Holy Grail special cup containing a drink that could make a person live forever

knight rich lord who fought for the king. Knights were called 'Sir'.

loyal to stand by someone no matter what happens

magic make-believe ability to do impossible things

nephew son of a person's brother or sister

rescued saved from harm

rule be in charge of a place and people

scabbard cover that a sword is kept in

wizard person who can do magic

Further Reading

Websites

Find out more about the Saxons in Britain at:
www.bbc.co.uk/schools/primaryhistory/anglo_saxons

Find out lots more about Arthur at:
www.kingarthursknights.com

Click to read the tale of Arthur or write your own story at:
www.primaryresources.co.uk/online/kingarthur.swf

Books

The Adventures of King Arthur
by Angela Wilkes, Usborne (2003).

The Sword in the Stone (Hopscotch Adventures)
by Karen Wallace, Franklin Watts (2006).

Index